YELP LOCAL MARKETING WORKBOOK:

HOW TO USE YELP FOR BUSINESS

2016 EDITION

BY JASON MCDONALD, PH.D.

© 2015-2016, JM INTERNET GROUP

https://www.jm-seo.org/

Tel. 800-298-4065

INTRODUCTION

Welcome to the *Yelp Local Marketing Workbook, 2016 edition!* Get ready to

- have some **fun**;
- **learn how Yelp, Google+ and other local review sites work;**
- understand how to use **Yelp, Google+ and other local review sites such as Google+** to **market your business**; and
- create a step-by-step **Yelp / Local marketing plan**.

Fully revised and updated for 2016, this workbook not only explains how to market on Yelp and other local review sites but also provides access to **free** Yelp / Local marketing tools. It provides overviews, step-by-step instructions, tips and secrets, free tools for Yelp / Local marketing, and (*wait, there's more!*) access to worksheets that will help you build a systematic Yelp / Local marketing plan. Even better, if you register your copy, you also get access to my complete *Social Media Toolbook*, with literally hundreds of free social media marketing tools to turbocharge your social media marketing not just on Yelp and other local review sites but also on LinkedIn, Twitter, YouTube, Google+, Instagram and other major social media platforms.

> *It slices, it dices. It explains how to Yelp works. It gives you free tools. And it helps you make a Yelp / Local marketing plan.*

If you're really gung-ho for **social media marketing**, I refer you to my *Social Media Workbook*, an all-in-one guide to the entire social media universe from Facebook to LinkedIn, Twitter to YouTube, Instagram to Pinterest, Yelp to Google+, and everything in between. Learn more about that book at http://jmlinks.com/social or call 800-298-4065.

Why Market via Yelp, Google+ and Local Review Sites?

If you've read this far, you're definitely intrigued by Yelp, Google+ and other local review sites as a marketing platform. Perhaps you're just starting out with a **Yelp or Google+ Listing** for your **business**. Or perhaps you already have a listing, but want to make it really work. Let's step back for a minute and ask: **why market on Yelp and other local review sites**?

Here are some reasons:

- **Local search is big.** Today's consumers go first to Google, Yelp, CitySearch and other local review sites for everything from restaurants to plumbers to divorce attorneys and to marriage counseling services.
- **Local is ubiquitous.** Nearly everyone uses local search and local review sites – from teenagers to grandmas, business executives to flight attendants. Gone are the days of the paper Yellow Pages. Here are the days of instant searches on mobile phones on Yelp, Google+ and other sites to find a nearby coffee shop or the best local surgeon for a facelift. From bail bonds to psychotherapists, from florists to doggie daycare, search and social has "gone local" and "gone review."
- **Yelp / Local is free for your business**. All of your major local review sites offer you the ability to "claim" and "optimize" your business listing. While you don't completely control your listing, there is still a lot you can do, for free, to build your brand, get to the top of local search on Yelp, Google, or Bing, and spread eWOM (electronic word of mouth), help you stay top-of-mind with your customers, and even "get shares" or "go viral."

Yelp and local search services, however, are also complicated. Using Yelp as a consumer is one thing, and marketing your business on Yelp, Google+, etc., is another. Most businesses fail at Yelp / Local marketing because they just don't "get it." They don't understand how Yelp and other local review sites work, and they fail to see the incredible marketing opportunities beneath the surface of the Review Revolution. Quite simply, you have to invest some time to learn "how" to market on Yelp and local review sites.

Enter the *Yelp Local Marketing Workbook*.

Who is this Workbook For?

This workbook is aimed primarily at **small business owners** and **marketing managers**. Non-profits will also find it useful.

If you are a person whose job involves advertising, marketing, and/or branding, this workbook is for you. If you are a small business that sees a marketing opportunity in local SEO, Yelp, local search on sites like Google+ or TripAdvisor, this workbook is for you. And if your job is to market a business or organization online in today's Internet economy, this book is for you. Anyone who wants to look behind the curtain and understand the mechanics of how to market on Yelp and other local review sites will benefit from this book.

Anyone who sees – however dimly – that Yelp could help market their business will benefit from this hands-on guide.

How Does This Workbook Work?

This workbook starts first with an overview to **social media *marketing***. If social media is a **party**, then **using social media** is akin to just *showing up*. **Marketing** on social media, in contrast, isn't about showing up. It's about ***throwing*** the party!

Understanding that distinction between "attending" the social media party and "throwing" the social media party is the subject of **Chapter One.**

Chapter Two is a deep dive into Yelp / Local marketing. We'll overview how Yelp and Google+ work, explain everything from unclaimed listings to claimed listings, reviewer profiles to the star rating systems, and how to cultivate positive reviews and react to negative reviews about your business online. It will all become much clearer, as we work through Yelp and other local review sites in plain English, written for "mere mortals." Along the way, I'll provide **worksheets** that will act as "Jason as therapist," so you can fill them out and begin to outline your own unique Yelp / Local marketing plan.

Finally, this workbook ends with an **Appendix**: a list of amazing **free Yelp / Local tools** and resources. Even better, if you register your copy, you get clickable online access to the tools, a PDF copy of the book, and (wait, there's more!) a complimentary copy of my *Social Media Toolbook*, my compilation of hundreds of social media tools not just for Yelp but for all the major platforms.

Here's how to register your copy of this workbook:

1. Go to https://jm-seo.org/workbooks
2. Click on Yelp / Local.
3. Use this password: **reviews2016**
4. You're in. Simply click on the link for a PDF copy of the *Social Media Toolbook* as well as access to the worksheets referenced herein.

OK, now that we know what this workbook is about, who it is for, and our plan of action...

Let's get started!

≫ MEET THE AUTHOR

My name is Jason McDonald, and I have been active on the Internet since 1994 (having invented the Internet along with Al Gore) and taught SEO, AdWords, and Social Media since 2009 – online, at Stanford University Continuing Studies, at both AcademyX and the Bay Area Video Coalition in San Francisco, at workshops, and in corporate trainings across these United States. I love figuring out how things work, and I love teaching others! Social media marketing is an endeavor that I understand, and I want to empower you to understand it as well.

Learn more about me at https://www.jasonmcdonald.org/ or at my corporate website https://www.jm-seo.org/. Or just call 800-298-4065, say something flattering, and I my secretary will put you through. *(Like I have a secretary! Just call if you have something to ask or say).*

≫ SPREAD THE WORD: WRITE A REVIEW & GET A FREE eBOOK!

If you like this workbook, please take a moment to write an honest review on Amazon.com. *If you hate the book, feel free to trash it on Amazon or anywhere across the Internet. (I have thick skin). If you hate life, in general, and are just one of those bitter people who write bitter reviews... well, gosh, go off and meditate, talk to a priest or do something spiritual. Life is just too short to be that bitter!*

At any rate, here is my special offer for those lively enough to write a review of the book–

1. Write your **honest review** on Amazon.com.
2. **Contact** me via https://www.jm-seo.org/contact and let me know your review is up.
3. Include your **email address** and **website URL**, and any quick questions you have about it.
4. I will send you a **free** copy of one of my other eBooks which cover AdWords, SEO, and Social Media Marketing.

This offer is limited to the first 100 reviewers, and only for reviewers who have purchased a paid copy of the book. You may be required to show proof of purchase and the birth certificate of your first born child, cat, or goldfish. If you don't have a child, cat, or goldfish, you may be required to prove telepathically that you bought the book.

▶▶ QUESTIONS AND MORE INFORMATION

I **encourage** my students to ask questions! If you have questions, submit them via https://www.jm-seo.org/contact/. There are two sorts of questions: ones that I know instantly, for which I'll zip you an email answer right away, and ones I do not know instantly, in which case I will investigate and we'll figure out the answer together.

As a teacher, I learn most from my students. So please don't be shy!

▶▶ COPYRIGHT AND DISCLAIMER

Uh! Legal stuff! Get ready for some fun:

This is a completely **unofficial** guide to Yelp marketing as well as marketing on other local review sites such as Google+, TripAdvisor, Airbnb, etc. Neither Yelp nor Google+ nor any other local review site has not endorsed this guide, nor has anyone affiliated with these sites been involved in the production of this guide.

That's a *good thing*. This guide is **independent**. My aim is to "tell it as I see it," giving you no-nonsense information on how to succeed at Yelp / Local marketing.

In addition, please note the following:

- All trademarks are the property of their respective owners. I have no relationship with nor endorsement from the mark holders. Any use of their marks is so I can provide information to you.

- Any reference to or citation of third party products or services whether for Facebook, LinkedIn, Twitter, Yelp, Google / Google+, Yahoo, Bing, Pinterest,

Amazon, YouTube, or other businesses, search engines, or social media platforms, should not be construed as an endorsement of those products or services tools, nor as a warranty as to their effectiveness or compliance with the terms of service with any search engine or social media platform.

The information used in this guide was derived in September, 2015. However, social media marketing changes rapidly, so please be aware that scenarios, facts, and conclusions are subject to change without notice.

Additional Disclaimer. Internet marketing is an art, and not a science. Any changes to your Internet marketing strategy, including SEO, Social Media Marketing, and AdWords, is at your own risk. Neither Jason McDonald, Excerpti Communications, Inc., nor the JM Internet Group assumes any responsibility for the effect of any changes you may, or may not, make to your website or AdWords advertising based on the information in this guide.

» ACKNOWLEDGEMENTS

No man is an island. I would like to thank my beloved wife, Noelle Decambra, for helping me hand-in-hand as the world's best moderator for our online classes, and as my personal cheerleader in the book industry. Gloria McNabb has done her usual tireless job as first assistant, including updating this edition as well the *Social Media Marketing* toolbook. Alex Facklis and Hannah McDonald also assisted with tools and research. I would also like to thank my black Labrador retriever, Buddy, for countless walks and games of fetch, during which I refined my ideas about marketing and about life.

And, again, a huge thank you to my students – online, in San Francisco, and at Stanford Continuing Studies. You challenge me, you inspire me, and you motivate me!

2

YELP / LOCAL

Let's suppose you have a restaurant, or you're a local plumber or dentist or divorce attorney or any of the thousands of local businesses that service customers in their day-to-day life. Before the advent of social media sites like Yelp, Google+, YP.com, TripAdvisor and their kind, consumers might have gone to the physical yellow pages or perhaps visited your website after a Google search. You were in charge of your marketing message: *customers couldn't really "talk back."*

The "Review Revolution" led by Yelp and since followed by Google+, YP.com, Angie's list, and other sites has dramatically changed the local landscape. Yelp made it possible for customers to "talk back," sharing their positive and negative reviews about local business across social media.

Reviews, in short, allow consumers to talk back: the good, the bad, and the ugly.

A happy customer can leave a **positive** review about your business, and a not-so-happy customer can leave a scathing **negative** review. Moreover, it's a fact that many (if not most) potential customers go online and check reviews before engaging with a local business. If they see five star or four star reviews on Yelp, they may reach out to your business with a phone call or email inquiry, or visit your restaurant, bar, or coffee shop. If they see two star or many negative reviews (perhaps even just one) on Yelp, Google+ or another local review site, they may skip over you and go to competitors who have better online reviews.

Online reviews, in short can make, or break, your business.

Using Yelp and Google+ as models, this chapter explores the "Review Revolution." First, we'll explore why and how customer reviews have dramatically changed the local business landscape. Second, we'll explore how to claim and optimize your listings on Yelp, Google+, and other review sites. Third, we'll investigate how reviews work and how you can nurture positive reviews about your business without getting into trouble. Finally, we'll finish up with a discussion of online reputation management.

Let's get started!

To Do List:

>> Explore How Review Sites Work

>> Inventory Companies on Yelp, Google+ or Other Relevant Sites

>> Claim and Optimize Your Listings

>> Cultivate Positive Reviews

>> Monitor and Improve Your Online Reputation

>> Measure your Results

>> Deliverable: a Yelp / Local Marketing Plan

>> Appendix: Top Ten Yelp / Local Review Marketing Tools and Resources

>> EXPLORE HOW REVIEW SITES WORK

The first big thing to grasp as a local business is the **Review Revolution** brought to us by Yelp in 2004. Imagine it's 1994, ten years prior to Yelp's founding, and you have a local Italian restaurant in Los Angeles, California. One day you are lucky enough to be visited by the review critic for the *Los Angeles Times*. You recognize her from her picture in the *LA Times*, and you realize that she can make – or break – your new Italian eatery. You do your best to not let her know you recognize who she is, and you do your utmost to ensure that she has a positive experience at your restaurant. One week later your hopes and prayers are answered: a positive restaurant review in the local newspaper. Business booms.

Alternatively, if she had written a critical review of your restaurant, business would not have *boomed*. It would have *busted*. **The review critic, in short, had an immense amount of power over local restaurants.** However, if a) you were a small restaurant you had minimal chance of ever getting reviewed, and b) if you were a divorce attorney, plumber, massage therapist, CPA or many other types of local businesses, there were essentially no reviewers available. Your main marketing channel was not reviews but customer word of mouth.

Enter the **Review Revolution**. In October, 2004, Yelp (http:www.yelp.com) was founded. Consumers of all types could now review not just local restaurants but local plumbers, dentists, massage therapists and thousands of other types of local businesses. The Review Revolution was like any other mass revolution: the masses burst open the doors of the castle, executed the ruling class, and turned over the table and chairs. *It was a bit bloody. It was a bit noisy. And it was a bit unpleasant.* If, for example, you were the *Los Angeles Times* restaurant critic, your absolute power over restaurants was broken. Professional critics, from restaurant reviewers to product reviewers to book reviewers, look on the review revolution with disgust.

The Review Revolution brought democracy to local reviews. Now anyone could review anything. No control: democracy arrived to reviews.

But here's the rub. Like the French Revolution, the Review Revolution brought the masses into the ecosystem. It has not been very organized or coherent; online reviews run the gamut from informative to ridiculous. Whereas the big reviewers of the *Los Angeles Times, San Francisco Chronicle*, and *New York Times* were educated and civilized (though they could be brutal in their reviews), the new review class can be rough and tumble. Anyone – and I do mean anyone – can write a review: good, bad, or ugly. To be frank, we are still living in this unsettled Review Revolution, and like the French Revolution, there is no going back: the old system is dead.

UNDERSTAND THE REVIEW REVOLUTION

If you're reading this chapter, you've probably already grasped that online reviews can make or break your local reviews. Many, if not all, potential customers consult online review sites like TripAdvisor, Yelp, or Google+ before engaging with local businesses. If they see *positive* reviews, they are primed for a *positive* experience. If they see *negative* reviews, they are so *negatively* primed that they may avoid any contact whatsoever with your business. Reviews now impact all types of local businesses; nearly every local business is being reviewed online 24/7 365.

Let's step back for a moment and understand the **review ecosystem**. With Yelp as the most important local review site, we will use Yelp as our model, and recognize that what's true for Yelp is generally true for all review sites because the all follow the same social media rules of engagement.

Here's how review sites work:

1. **Local businesses have profiles**. Business profiles are created *without the permission or participation of the business owner*, and exist whether or not the business owner has claimed, optimized, and participated in the review ecosystem. *You as the business owner do not have the right to "delete" your listing on Yelp!* It's like a business Page on Facebook, to the extent that your business has on online "Page" on Yelp. But unlike on Facebook, you are not in control.
2. **Customers write reviews**. Registered Yelp users are able to write reviews about any local business they choose. *If your business is not listed, Yelp users can even create a listing for your business and then review it.* These reviews may be good or bad, extremely positive or so negatively scathing as to infuriate you as the business owner. The Yelpers are basically in control.
3. **Customers establish a reputation**. The more reviews a customer writes, the older his or her profile as a reviewer on Yelp, the more friends on Yelp, the more thumbs up or thumbs down to their reviews, the stronger their profile gets. Yelp has filters to filter out "fake" or "weak" reviews from showing entirely. The stronger the customer profile, the higher their reviews rise on the pages of those businesses that they have reviewed. Your business and the Yelpers are both simultaneously establishing a reputation, and that reputation impacts whether your information (your listing, their review) shows prominently on Yelp. (Remember: the same is true for Google+, TripAdvisor, Airbnb, and even Amazon).
4. **Prospective customers read reviews**. Potential customers visit sites like Yelp, CitySearch, TripAdvisor, Google+, and search for businesses via keywords. They find businesses of interest and read the reviews. Generally speaking, if they find positive reviews, they are primed to engage with that business. If they find negative reviews, they may not so much as even call or visit the business. Good reviews can propel your business dramatically forward. Bad reviews can literally kill your business. The stakes are high!
5. **Businesses claim their local listings**. Businesses have the right to claim, and optimize, their listings. By claiming their listing on a site like Yelp, the business can "optimize" it by improving the business description with accurate keywords, uploading photos, responding to reviews, and in some cases like Google+ post

updates. While businesses cannot delete their listings nor their negative reviews, they can participate in the new social media ecosystem of reviews.

For an overview to Yelp by Yelp, visit http://www.yelp-support.com/. For your first TODO, sign up for a Yelp account (as a consumer not a business) if you do not already have one. Next, go to Yelp (http://www.yelp.com/) to explore some of the following categories in your local city by typing these keywords into the Yelp search box:

Sushi Restaurants

Jazz

Plumbers

Divorce Attorneys

DUI Attorneys

Bail Bonds

Let's take Bail Bonds, for example. Here's a screenshot of how to search for "bail bonds" near San Francisco, CA:

Use the clickable links below to do the search:

- Here's a search for "Bail Bonds" near San Francisco, CA at http://jmlinks.com/4i.
- And here's one of the top search results: *New Century Bail Bonds* http://jmlinks.com/4j

Here are some things to notice about the *New Century Bail Bonds* listing.

First, scroll down about half way and look for "From the business" in red. It starts with "JAIL SUCKS." This is the **business listing**, as edited and submitted by the business. This indicates that this business has claimed their listing. Note the inclusion of relevant keywords, the types of search queries a users might type into Yelp.

Second, notice the **photos** at the top of the listing (http:jmlinks.com/4k). These can be submitted either by the business, or by users. So, if you don't submit some, your users might (and they might be favorable, or unfavorable, to your business).

Third, read some of the **reviews**. Notice that for any individual reviewer, Yelp indicates how many friends they have on Yelp and how many reviews they have written. For example, here is a screenshot of one of the reviews, showing two friends and two reviews:

Tonya T.
San Leandro, CA
2 friends
2 reviews

 12/23/2013

Would like to take a moment to send a HUGE THANK YOU to Tiki Maxwell and her team at Bail Now Bail Bonds for doing an excellent job with my brother's bond.

Tiki did a fantastic job of being very clear and precise with regards to the details of my brothers charges as well as keeping us up to date regarding the status of his case, as well as upcoming court dates. She remained professional, however was extremely compassionate and sympathetic regarding my family's situation.

Fourth, click on a **reviewer photo**, and you'll go up to their **Yelp profile**. For example, click on Tonya T (http://jmlinks.com/4l) and you'll go up to her profile. Read her reviews and make a guess as to how "real" and how "unsolicited" her reviews are. Some reviewers will look very legitimate, and others might look solicited, paid, or even faked. You'll soon realize that Yelp, like all the review-based sites, is a hodgepodge of unsolicited and solicited reviews, real and fake reviews, and so on and so forth.

For example, here's a screen shot of a suspicious review:

Notice how Chloe D, has *zero* friends, has written only *one* review, lives in *Manhattan* and yet reviewed a *San Francisco* Bail Bonds. Is this a real review? A solicited review? Or a faked review?

Fifth, scroll to the very bottom and click on "review that are not currently recommended." Yelp has a filter that attempts to filter out "fake" reviews and filter in "real reviews." Here's a screenshot:

Read some of these "non-recommended" reviews and attempt to guess which ones are truly real and which ones might be fake. Do you think Yelp is doing a good, or bad job, with its filter? How do the reviews shown prominently compare or contrast with the reviews at the bottom, or the reviews that are hidden?

Compare Yelp to Amazon

Reviews do not exist only on Yelp, however. Take any review site and do the same exercise.

For instance, check out some reviews on Amazon, as a contrast to Yelp, by clicking on http://jmlinks.com/4m and http://jmlinks.com/4n. Notice how many reviews these people are writing; read their reviews. Do they look fake to you? Perhaps paid or solicited? Realize that all the review sites – Yelp, CitySearch, Google+, Amazon – have essentially the same structure: profiles of businesses, reviewers with profiles, reviews by reviewers rated by stars, a filtering system, and a search process generated by user search queries and showing the "best" results based on keywords in their description and in their reviews, geographic proximity to the searcher, and number or quality of reviews.

Is this fair? Is it a better opportunity for your business than in 1994 when there were no online reviews? Whether it's fair or not, good or not, is a different issue than how you as a local business can (and should) play the game of local reviews to win. You do not make the review world: you simply live in it.

LIFE IS NOT FAIR. NEITHER ARE REVIEWS.

None of this is perfect, and I am not singling out Yelp. I am drawing your attention to the Review Revolution and the fact that it is not just real people spontaneously reviewing businesses but rather a mix of people writing spontaneous real reviews, people writing solicited (yet real) reviews, and even fake people writing fake reviews.

Users Believe Reviews

Users believe online reviews! According to a BrightLocal study, fully 92% of consumers now read online reviews (vs. 88% in 2014), and 68% say positive reviews make them trust a local business more (vs. 72% in 2014). You can read the full study at http://jmlinks.com/5b. Another excellent book on the social aspects of the Review Revolution is Bill Tancer's, *Everyone's a Critic*, at http://www.billtancer.com/.

The reality is the users believe reviews, both good and bad, and both real and faked. The review ecosystem is a mess, yet as a business owner you have to realize (and accept) that reviews of all types impact your business. You can't change this fact; you can only work within the new "rules of the game."

That's the reality of the Review Revolution.

Is it fair that many consumers are not sufficiently skeptical about the reviews they read? No.

Is it fair that Yelp, Amazon, Google+, TripAdvisor and other vendors are not doing as much as they could to filter out fake reviews as well as address the lopsided problem that the most likely unsolicited review is often a negative one? No.

Do any of these companies care about your business or the fact that you now live within the Review Revolution? No.

Is life fair? No. Is the Review Revolution fair? No.

Do both life and the review revolution offers fabulous opportunities despite their flaws? Yes, yes, yes!

Unhappy Small Business Owners

In my face-to-face classes on social media, review sites are among the most controversial. Yelp, in particular, is literally hated by many small businesspeople because a) they have received what they think are unfair negative reviews on Yelp, and b) Yelp has a reputation for strong-arming businesses into paid advertising. (Yelp disputes this charge, though rumors have dogged the company for years).

Here's why local businesses often get quite emotional about sites like Yelp:

1. Often times, the only reviews they have about their business are negative reviews, which they feel are inaccurate or unfair.
2. They do not understand how to claim or optimize their listings, nor how to respond to reviews.
3. They do not understand how reviews work, and how to influence reviews in their favor.

Moreover, many small business owners do not step back and compare 2016 with 1994. Then, only the rich, famous, connected, or lucky got reviews in the local papers. Getting reviewed was like winning the lottery: great if it happened in a positive way, but not something upon which you could build a marketing strategy. Today, however, any business can get reviews, and consumers can read those reviews online. The reality is that the Review Revolution created an enormous **positive marketing opportunity** for your business.

Let me repeat that:

The Review Revolution created an enormous positive marketing opportunity for your business!

If you know how to use it (more on that later).

Who Writes Reviews?

Let's talk about who writes reviews. Let's get real. Let's assume you are a local plumber. I have a clogged toilet. I go online and find your business. You come out, you fix my toilet, and you give me a bill for $300. You did a good job, and I am happy about the service.

Will I go online to Yelp and write a review? It's doubtful. Unlike my relationship with a local prestige restaurant, I am not "proud" that I have a leaky toilet and I got it fixed. I am not "excited" that you provided me with excellent service. Therefore, as a happy customer, I am unlikely to leave a positive review.

My toilet has been fixed. I'm happy. Done. Over. End. Writing a review is the last thing on my mind.

Now, let's say you come out for my toilet repair, and you do NOT do what I consider a good job. Perhaps you crack my tile floor, or perhaps you get dirty water on my rug, or perhaps I just don't like you, or perhaps I find your fee of $300 unreasonable.

I'm mad. I hate you. I pay the bill. I'm angry and I want revenge.

I think to myself, "I'll show you." I go online, and vent my anger in a Yelp review. I explain to fellow Yelpers (and the world) how terrible you are, how they should never use your business, etc. etc. I do this to "let off steam" as well as to "feel good about myself" that I am "doing the world a favor" by righting the wrong of your terrible business. I want you to go out of business. I want you to fail. That's justice to me, the unhappy customer.

(Don't believe this happens? To read reviews of the "worst food of my life" on Yelp, visit http://jmlinks.com/4z; to read reviews of the "best food of my life" on Yelp, visit http://jmlinks.com/5a.) You'll see both good, and bad, reviews on Yelp.

Two scenarios: a positive experience, and a negative experience.

Here's the **dirty little secret** of the review ecosystem (with the possible exception of entertainment venues like restaurants, bars, museums, etc.):

- The **most likely customer to leave an unsolicited review is the unhappy customer.** The very unhappy customer is very likely to spontaneously write a nasty review about your business.
- **Happy customers are NOT likely to write reviews**. They are not pre-motivated to share their experience with your plumbing company, your CPA firm, your DUI attorney services on Yelp without a nudge from you. (For restaurants, bars, and entertainment-type businesses, happy customers are much more likely to leave reviews.)

Two other customer segments are likely to leave reviews.

- **Review geeks / Extreme Yelpers** – which would be people like myself, digitally connected and participatory in the Yelp (or Google+, TripAdvisor) ecosystems. Review geeks are not necessarily primed to leave positive, or negative reviews. They just tend to review frequently. As Yelp has evolved, more and more people ARE leaving reviews spontaneously about local services, which is a good thing.
- The **hostile minority** - these are unhappy campers who, because of sites like Yelp, now have a way to vent their rage at nearly everything. These "unhappy campers" tend to leave unhappy review after unhappy review: bitter and negative, they tend to hate everything and leave a destructive trail of negative reviews in their wake. Unfortunately without any fault on its part, Yelp enabled the very unhappy, bitter people of the world to spread their negativity by venting against businesses. Don't believe me? Try some Yelp searches, look for negative reviews,

and click "up" to the profiles of the reviewers. In just a few minutes, I guarantee that you will find some very negative, pathetic sad little people.

UNHAPPY CUSTOMERS OFTEN WRITE REVIEWS

Yelp was built around restaurants, the one case in which satisfied customers are likely to leave reviews. Why? To show "to the world" that they have the disposable income and prestige to dine out. Similar to what you see on Facebook, people like to "showcase" their positive achievements. *Look at me! I went to Disneyland, I went out to dinner, I went to this amazing museum, ate at this exclusive restaurant.*

Still, even in the entertainment sectors, unhappy customers are very likely to leave reviews.

The takeway here is to realize the following:

> *If you do nothing, the most likely reviews you will get will be negative reviews.*

Let me repeat that because it is incredibly important to understand the dirty little secret of the Review Revolution:

> *If you do nothing, the most likely reviews you will get will be negative reviews.*

Official Policy

It gets worse. The official policies of Yelp, Google+, TripAdvisor and the like is that you – as the business owner – are not allowed to solicit reviews in any way shape or fashion. Yelp, for example, advises business owners:

Don't ask your customers to review your business on Yelp. Over time, solicited reviews create bias in your business listing — a bias that savvy consumers can smell from a mile away. (Source: http://jmlinks.com/4g).

TripAdvisor states as follows:

The following actions may be considered fraudulent:

– Attempts by an owner to boost his/her own property's reputation by:

- *Writing a review for his/her own property*
- *Asking friends or relatives to write positive reviews*
- *Submitting a review on behalf of a guest*
- *Copying comment cards and submitting them as reviews*
- *Pressuring a TripAdvisor member to remove a negative review*
- *Offering incentives such as discounts, upgrades, or any special treatment in exchange for reviews*
- *Hiring an optimization company, third party marketing organization, or anyone to submit false reviews*
- *Impersonating a competitor or a guest in any way*

– Attempts by an owner to damage his/her competitors by submitting a negative review.

Bottom line: Any attempt to mislead, influence or impersonate a traveler is considered fraudulent and will be subject to penalty. (Source: http://jmlinks.com/4h).

The Review Dilemma

So here's the **review dilemma**:

- **On the one hand,** if you do nothing, you are very likely to receive negative reviews from unhappy customers and not so likely to receive positive reviews from happy customers (true in all cases, except perhaps entertainment-type industries), but

- *On the other hand,* the official terms of service forbid you from soliciting reviews from customers.

Damned if you do, damned if you don't.

The reality of the Review Revolution is that in most cases and certainly in competitive industries like divorce law, DUI cases, plumbers, roofers, etc., most successful companies are pro-actively soliciting reviews. This does not mean that they are faking or buying reviews; it only means that they are nudging, cajoling, begging, emotionally incentivizing, and otherwise motivating happy customers to go online and take the time to write positive reviews around their business.

Is this fair? No.

Is this in accord with the terms of service? No.

Is it the reality? Yes.

Is it the public reality? No. Yelp, Google+, TripAdvisor, Amazon, and all the other companies do their best to police reviews, but the reality is that the fact that reviews are heavily manipulated by vendors is an open secret.

But wait a second.

Is life fair? No.

Was it likely that your plumbing company would have been reviewed in the paper in 1995? No. Your small restaurant? No.

Even though the posted speed limit on the highway is 60 mph, do most cars actually go 60 mph? No.

The Review Revolution has given you an enormous, positive opportunity to reach new customers, just like the Interstate Highway System gives you the opportunity to travel cross-country at 65 to 80 mph even though the posted speed limit may by 75 mph (in the West) and 60 mph (in the East).

> *Don't be the fastest car on the road. Don't be the red Mazda Miata going 95 mph in front of the cop. Just be in the fast car group, just not the fastest, most egregious car.*

For now, just understand that positive reviews are the key to success, that soliciting reviews is technically against the terms of service, and begin to realize that you are going to have to create a strategy to solicit positive reviews, despite the posted terms of service.

Let's turn, first, to identifying companies to emulate on the various review sites.

» INVENTORY COMPANIES ON YELP, GOOGLE+ OR OTHER RELEVANT SITES

If you are a local business, it will be pretty obvious that reviews matter. Even if you are a national business, you may realize that reviews matter. Your first step therefore is to identify the review sites that matter to your business. Your second step is to then browse similar businesses on those sites and conduct an inventory of what you like and dislike about their listings, realizing that unlike on Facebook, listings on review sites generally occur with or without the permission of the business. Actual control is much more limited.

Among the most important review sites are:

> Yelp (http://www.yelp.com/) – the largest local review site with great strength in restaurants, more popular in "Blue" states like New York or California than in "Red" states like Florida or Texas.

> Google+ (http://www.google.com/). Accessibly by doing Google searches on relevant keywords. In some cases, you'll need to first find a company, and then Google its name to find its Google+ page (more below).

> TripAdvisor (http://www.tripadvisor.com/). The leading travel review site.

> YP (http://www.yp.com/). The traditional yellow pages gone digital.

VRBO (http://www.vrbo.com/) – a site for identifying short term vacation rentals.

Airbnb (http://www.airbnb.com/) – the leading site for vacation rentals.

Amazon (http://www.amazon.com/) – earth's largest retailer, with reviews on billions of products.

GlassDoor (http://www.glassdoor.com/) – reviews about businesses from the perspective of employees.

IDENTIFY COMPANIES WHO DO REVIEW MARKETING WELL, AND REVERSE ENGINEER THEM

The easiest way to find logical review sites for your company is as follows:

1. Identify the **keywords** by which prospective customers might search for you. For example, if you are a Sushi restaurant in San Francisco, those keywords might be words such as "Sushi," "Sushi Bar," "Japanese Restaurant," "Japanese Caterers," etc.
2. **Google** those keywords and note which review sites come up.
3. Click over to the listing sites, and **make a list** of them.
4. Go over to each review site, re-input your search query keywords, and begin to browse company listings on the review site(s) you have identified.

For example, take "vacation rentals Lake Tahoe" and search it on Google (http://jmlinks.com/4p). Then, browse the search results and you'll see:

https://www.flipkey.com/

http://www.homeaway.com/

http://www.vrbo.com/

http://www.tripadvisor.com/

https://www.tahoeaccomodations.com/

http://www.vacationrentals.com/

https://www.airbnb.com/

Obviously the sites returned will vary with your keywords. By using this technique, however, you can use Google to identify the most important review sites and directories in your industry. Your TODOS here are

1. Take out a piece of paper, or set up a Word or Google document. Title this "keyword list."
2. Using tools like the Google *keyword planner*, Google *suggest* (the terms suggested by Google when you type), or Google *related searches* (the terms that appear at the very bottom of the page) as well as just brainstorming "how customers might search for you," create a keyword list of relevant terms. (To watch a video on how to use the Keyword Planner, visit http://jmlinks.com/5c, and to watch a video on how to build a Keyword Worksheet, visit http://jmlinks.com/5d).
3. Conduct these searches on Google, and create an organize list of relevant search queries customers might use on Google, Yelp, etc.
4. As you search, write down the top review / directory sites that come up. Build a list of relevant review sites in your industry.

You now have an organized list of which reviews sites matter to you and your business. This list will, of course, be different for a *Bed and Breakfast* vs. a *CPA* vs. a *divorce attorney* vs. a *sushi restaurant*, but the review marketing game has the same rules across all review sites.

Google+ is Special

Among listing and review sites, Google+ is special. First and foremost, it's owned and operated by Google and has clear priority on Google search. Having a strong Google+ local presence is the No. 1 way for your business to show on local-related Google searches. It doesn't take much to look forward and realize that if local matters to you, and your customers use Google, you'll need to optimize your Google+ local listing!

However, Google has done a **terrible** job of managing Google+ local (now renamed to Google My Business (https://www.google.com/business). Here's how to find companies to browse on Google+.

Method #1: Use Google

- Go to https://www.google.com/.
- Enter a relevant keyword such as "Pizza Tulsa Oklahoma"
- Make a list of the top company names showing in the results of the Google+ box (usually showing at the top with the stars), for example: "Joe Momma's Tulsa"
  - If the company has at least one review, then click on the blue "Google Reviews" link.
    - Click on the name or photo of one of the reviewers.
    - Scroll down and find the company you want to browse by name.
    - Click on the company name. This is their "Google+ page" and you'll be able to see their reviews, about tab, and posts if any exist.
  - If the company has zero reviews, it's quite a bit harder.
    - Go back to Google, and type in site:plus.google.com Joe Mommas Tulsa as for example http://jmlinks.com/4r, meaning *site:plus.google.com competitor's name city name*
    - Browse until you find a Google+ page that includes an "about" tab with reviews.

Method #2: Use Google+ Brand Pages Search.

- Go to http://www.gpluspagesearch.com/
- Enter competitor business names and then click over to their Google+ pages/

Note: it does NOT work very well for keywords, so use this method ONLY for competitor names.

Method #3: Use Google Site Search

- Go to Google.com
- Enter site:plus.google.com and then your competitor name. For example, here's site:plus.google.com "Mazzios Pizza" (a Tulsa Pizza Chain) at http://jmlinks.com/4q.
- Browse the listings. You may have to bounce around a while to find the Google+ page of a competitor.

At the time of writing, it's pretty clear that major changes are underway at Google+. It's even conceivable that Google will abandon Google+ entirely and move to some other sort of local / review system. No one knows for certain. What is certain is that Google controls search, and that many customers search Google, find companies, and click on reviews BEFORE they take any action.

If local matters to you, you must master Google+!

Inventory Companies and Their Local Listings

As you browse local review sites, identify relevant companies and make a list of their listings on Yelp, Google+ local, or other sites that are relevant. Make note of:

- Does their **listing** appear **claimed**?
- **Photos**: cover photos and profile pictures. Do you like what you see? Why or why not?
- **Reviews**. How many reviews do they have? Are the mostly positive or mostly negative? Click on the reviewers. Do they seem "real"? Unsolicited? Solicited? Faked? Try to reverse engineer how they might be soliciting or encouraging reviews.
- **About Tab**. Check out their about tab, or listing. Read it. Do you like how it's written? Does it include relevant keywords?

For your second TODO, download the **Review Research Worksheet**. For the worksheet, go to https://www.jm-seo.org/workbooks (click on Yelp / Local, enter the code 'reviews2016' to register if you have not already done so), and click on the link to the "Reviews Research Worksheet." You'll answer questions as to whether your potential customers are using reviews, which review sites are important, and inventory what you like and dislike about their review marketing set up and marketing strategy.

▶▶ CLAIM AND OPTIMIZE YOUR LISTINGS

Now that you've identified which local review sites matter, it's time to claim and optimize your listings. All of the sites work in essentially the same way, although there are differences in the details. The basic steps are:

1. Identify the local review site for which you want to "claim" your company listing.
2. Find your listing on the site.
3. Follow the instructions to "claim" it, usually by phone or postcard verification.
4. Optimize your listing description by writing keyword-heavy text, uploading photographs, and populating your listing with your hours of operation and other details.
5. Make sure that your website links back to your listing, and your listing links to your website.
6. Make sure that the business name, address, and phone number are the same on both the listing site and your website (be consistent).

To do this for Yelp:

1. Go to http://biz.yelp.com/
2. Enter your business name, and address and hit **Get Started** in red.
3. Follow the instructions to claim your business, usually by phone verification.
4. Once you have claimed your listing:
   a. Click on Business Information on the left; re-write your description to contain logical keywords that potential customers might search for, including synonyms (*pizza, Italian restaurant, catering*, for example).
   b. Choose relevant categories from the list provided.
   c. Enter your basic information, hours, specialties (business information), history, and "meet the business owner" with an eye to logical keywords.
   d. Click on photos on the left, and upload nice photos.
5. Make sure that the address and phone on Yelp are the SAME as the address and phone on your website.

6. Make sure that your website links to your Yelp listing (usually in the footer), and that your Yelp listing links to your website.

To do this for Google+:

1. Sign in to your Google account or Gmail (if you use Gmail).
2. Go to https://www.google.com/business
3. Click on the blue "Get your page" link on the top right.
4. Choose the "Storefront" or "Service Area" as indicated. A "storefront" sees customers at its own location; a "service area" is like a plumber or roofing company that goes out to see customers at their homes.
5. Enter your business name and address.
6. Follow the instructions to claim your business, usually by postcard verification.
7. When you get the postcard, enter the PIN as indicated in the instructions.
8. Optimize your business description by clicking on the red "edit" button.'
9. Choose relevant categories.
10. Click on "manage photos" to change your profile picture, and cover photos, as well as add interior and/or exterior photos.
11. Make sure that the address and phone on Google+ are the SAME as the address and phone on your website.
12. Make sure that your website links to your Google+ listing (usually in the footer), and that your Yelp listing links to your website.

Other local listings like YP.com or Citysearch follow similar procedures. To find all of your "second tier" listings, you can go to Yext (http://www.yext.com/) and enter your business name and phone number in the box on the right. Here's a screenshot:

For free, Yext will identify all your local listings. You can then click over to each and claim and optimize each. Or, if you have budget, you can subscribe to Yext and they will do this for all local listings including Yelp but EXCLUDING Google+. A competitive service to Yext is MOZ Local at https://moz.com/local.

Citation Consistency and Google Local Searches

To show up on Google search, it is important that ALL review sites and your website have the SAME company name, the SAME phone number, and SAME physical address. Make sure that your company name, phone number, and physical address appear on your website, usually in the footer.

"Citation" refers to the external listings on review websites that confirm (to Google and Bing) that your business has a certain phone number and physical address. This is used by the search engines to filter local search results by their proximity to the searcher or the geographic terms used in the search query.

Using a service like Yext allows you to claim, optimize, and make consistent this information across hundreds of review sites. This consistency is a big help to showing at the top of local searches on Google or Bing / Yahoo.

ToDo

For your third ToDo, make a spreadsheet of ALL relevant local review sites. Go to each, and claim / optimize your local listings. Be sure to note your login and password!

- CLAIM YOUR GOOGLE+ AND YELP WITH A PERMANENT CORPORATE EMAIL (NOT AN EMPLOYEE EMAIL)
- DO NOT LOSE YOUR GOOGLE+ AND YELP LOGIN AND PASSWORDS!

Lost password retrieval on Yelp and Google+ is a **disaster**! Neither system has a good password retrieval function; on Yelp in particular, if your password is lost, God help you. Do not lose your passwords.

» CULTIVATE POSITIVE REVIEWS

We'll assume you've claimed and optimized the relevant listing services for your local business. Most often this will be at least Google+ and Yelp, and in specific industries it might include TripAdvisor, VRBO, or Airbnb. If you sell products, it might be your product listings and uploads on Amazon. Or it might be on Glassdoor.com.

At this point, you have two options:

1. Wait **passively** for positive customer reviews, and hope that the positive reviews will outpace the negative reviews (according to the official policy of Yelp, Google+, etc.).
2. Be **pro-active** and try to encourage your happy customers to post reviews.

Which do you think the winners in local search and social media are doing?

Legal Disclaimer

You are responsible for everything you do in terms of your Internet marketing. Nothing I am writing here should be construed as required or recommended advice. Legally, I am recommending that you do nothing (option #1).

Take responsibility for your own actions as a marketer, and act on your own risk!

Soliciting Reviews

That said, here is the reality. If you wait passively for reviews (unless you are in the entertainment industry like a restaurant or bar), the most likely scenarios will be a) no reviews, or b) bad reviews, or at least a preponderance of bad reviews. The reason for this is if a customer's plumbing experience is good, she's happy and she goes on with her life. If her plumbing experience is bad, however, she might get angry and be motivated to go on Yelp, Google+, CitySearch, etc., and "tell the world" about how much she hates the company that did her wrong.

> *This dynamic is the dirty little secret of review marketing: unhappy customers are the ones most likely to leave unsolicited reviews.*

You the business owner or marketer can, however, fight back against this dynamic. Here are some strategies to solicit positive reviews about your business:

Face to Face. This is the most powerful way to get positive reviews. The employee who is "face to face" with the customer builds rapport with customer. A scenario might be:

> *Technician: "OK, I've fixed your toilet. Let's run through it together, and verify it's in working order.*
>
> *Client: Yes, it's great. Thank you so much!*
>
> *Technician: You're welcome. Hey, if you have a moment, could you do us a HUGE FAVOR and write a review on Google+ or Yelp about your experience?*
>
> *Client: Yes.*

- If client knows how to do this, just give him or her a card with a direct link to the review site location.
- If client does not know how to do this, give him or her a card with step-by-step instructions.

Phone Reminders. Either at the time of service, or shortly thereafter, call the customer to see "how it went," and if they're happy, ask them to write a review online.

Paper Reminders. Either at the time of service, or shortly thereafter, mail a physical postcard thanking the client for their business, and asking them to write a review on Yelp, Google+, etc.

Email Reminders. Either at the time of service, or shortly thereafter, send an email thanking the client for their business, and asking them to write a review online.

The reality is that face-to-face is, by far, the strongest way to motivate customers to write reviews, phone contact the next strongest, and so on and so forth.

Help Customers Write Reviews

Many customers may not understand how to write a review, so a step-by-step instruction sheet would be helpful. Use a URL shortener like http://bit.ly, or http://tinyurl.com to shorten the link to your local review listing page.

You can write this in an email or on a printed sheet of paper. Here's an example of an email I might send to my clients:

Greetings!

Thank you so much for the opportunity to serve your Internet marketing and consulting needs. As the owner of the *Jason McDonald SEO Consulting Agency*, I truly appreciate your business!

If you have a moment, I would REALLY appreciate an honest review on one of the local listing sites. Here are the instructions:

Google+.

1. Sign in to your Google and/or Gmail account at https://www.google.com/.
2. Go to http://bit.ly/review-jason.
3. Click on the white "Write a review"
4. Write your review

Yelp:

1. Sign into your Yelp account at http://www.yelp.com/.
2. Go to http://bit.ly/jason-yelp.
3. Click on the red "write a review" button
4. Write your review

Thank you,

Jason McDonald

TO GET POSITIVE REVIEWS, ASK HAPPY CUSTOMERS TO REVIEW YOU.

A few free services have tools to help you create nice-looking Web pages and handouts to encourage reviews:

Bright Local at http://jmlinks.com/4s.

WhiteSpark at http://jmlinks.com/4t.

Be Judicious. Understand "Plausible Deniability"

Understand that according to the official policy, even a mild handout asking for an "honest review" is a violation of the terms of service of most of the review providers! Therefore, I do NOT recommend that you post these publically on your website. Be judicious: give them out in printed or email format, and only to those happy customers who have been pre-selected by your staff.

Obviously, if a client is unhappy and you cannot fix it to make them happy: DO NOT ASK THEM FOR A REVIEW.

In fact, a really smart strategy is as follows:

- **Conduct a survey** of customers after they use your service asking them a) if they are happy, b) if they would write a review, and c) if they know how. This could be done formally (an email survey on a site like Surveymonkey (http://www.surveymonkey.com)) or informally just be pre-asking the customer face-to-face, over the phone, or via email.
- **If they ARE happy**, then ask them nicely to **write a review**.
- **If they are NOT happy**, either a) make them happy, or b) do **NOT** ask them for a review.

In this way, you avoid motivating unhappy customers to review you online. Indeed, if you are in a sensitive industry (e.g., Bail Bonds, apartment rentals) in which many customers are not happy, I do not recommend you even publicize to your clients face-to-face or in the real world that you are on the review sites. If many of your customers will be negative, then do not make it "easy" for them to give you a negative review!

Paying for Reviews

Let's face it. Review marketing is the "contact sport" of social media marketing. In certain industries (e.g., DUI attorneys, private detectives, breast augmentation services), many reviews are solicited if not faked, and sometimes incentivized with monetary incentives.

Should you pay for reviews? Generally speaking, I would not pay for reviews. (I am talking about real clients not completely faked reviews). Some companies do incentivize by giving $25 Starbucks or Amazon gift cards once a review is published; however, if this becomes known to a Yelp or a Google+ you wrong a very strong risk of being severely penalized.

Offering monetary incentives to get reviews is a dangerous strategy, so be forewarned.

Yelp will even mark your listing with an aggressive naughty notice if you are busted paying for reviews. You can browse real examples of this on Yelp at http://jmlinks.com/4u. First and foremost, therefore, if you choose to "go to the dark side" and offer payments, I would not publicize it! And I AM NOT RECOMMENDING THAT YOU DO THIS. I am just pointing out that it is done.

Completely faked reviews are also purchased online at sites like Fiverr (http://www.fiverr.com), but I do NOT recommend this strategy. If your business does not have a cohort of happy customers who will review you with just a face-to-face ask, then you have more serious issues than review marketing. So fix the business first, and then start asking happy real customers for reviews.

Incentivize Employees

A better way to incentivize is to offer your employees an incentive, rather than the customer, for reviews published online. Assume for example you are a local pizza joint. Offer your employees a $25.00 bonus EACH after each positive review on Yelp. Or if you are a roofing company, give the technician a handout explaining how to write a review online, and give him a $25.00 bonus EACH TIME a customer posts a review. In that way, you motivate your front-line employees to be customer-friendly, and when there is a positive customer experience, to politely ask the customer to write an honest review on Yelp, Google+, etc.

Motivate your employees to ask for reviews!

I would not put any pro-active review solicitation strategy in writing on the Internet, just as I would not call the California Highway Patrol and inform them that, in general, I go five miles faster than the posted speed limit while driving the highways and byways of the Golden State.

Let sleeping dogs lie.

But just as going 65 mph in a 60 mph zone is unlikely to cause a police action, polite nudges to encourage real reviews from real customers are unlikely to be a big problem. If you do it, just keep it private.

In my experience, if most businesses would simply ask a few clients for reviews, they would get them. Yes, you'll ask ten clients to get one review. But you'll get that one review. The real problem is to motivate employees to ask and ask and ask and ask to get that one review to go live on Yelp, Google+, or other review sites.

Recognize, understand, and accept that you will ask ten people to get just one review. That's just how it is: customers are self-centered and lazy (but we love them).

Why Reviews Matter (a Lot)

Getting positive reviews is hard work. It's not done in a day. Slow and steady will win the race. Just create a culture at your business of great customer service and an awareness of that "special moment" when a customer is happy to ask for a positive honest review.

Reviews, however, are worth their weight in **gold**. No, in **platinum**. Here's why:

1. **Reviews are a "trust indicator."** For better or worse, consumers tend to believe reviews and use them as trust indicators about your business. A company that has many positive reviews will crush a company that has negative reviews, and outperform a company that has just a few or zero reviews.
2. **Reviews help you in search.** The MORE reviews you have the HIGHER you will show at the top of Google, Yelp, CitySearch, TripAdvisor, Amazon, and even iTunes!

REVIEWS ARE WORTH THEIR WEIGHT IN PLATINUM

Do anything and everything honestly and ethically possible to encourage your best customers to "spread the word" by writing reviews about your business online. After just a few positive reviews, you will be amazed at what they do for your business.

Responding to Negative Reviews

Negative reviews will happen. As the business owner, you may feel as if someone walked up to your newborn baby sleeping calmly in her stroller and said to you:

Your baby is ugly. Your baby stinks. I hate your baby. I had a bad experience with your baby, and I am going to tell the world how much the baby that you are working for blood, sweat, and tears is terrible.

You're human. You're close to your business. It is like your baby. Your first reaction will be **ANGER**.

Resist the temptation to respond in kind. Do not go online and argue with the negative consumer. Do not insult them. Do not use unprofessional language. *When you wrestle with a pig, the pig gets dirty and the pig likes it.*

Instead:

- **Calm down**. Wait at least 24 hours before doing anything. Sleep on it.
- **Have someone else deal with negative reviews**: an outside consultant or employee who is not emotionally involved. Let a calm head prevail, and it probably will not be the head of the business owner.
- **Try to fix the problem**. If at all possible, reason with the person (you can usually contact them via Yelp, Google+, etc.), and see if you can fix the problem. In some cases, you can, and then you can politely ask them to change the review.
- **Respond**. State your side of the situation in a positive, professional manner while acknowledging the right of the reviewer to her own opinion.

To **respond to a negative review**, do as follows. First and foremost, take the high ground. You can log into your business account / profile and respond to negative reviews. This is one of the benefits of "claiming" your business profile. But be positive and professional: acknowledge their right to their opinion, but be firm as to your right to state your opinion as well. Second, state your side of the situation but realize you are NOT talking to the unhappy customer. You are talking to the person reading your reviews and deciding whether to reach out to you for a possible business engagement. Explain your side of the story. Often times, the negative reviews come from nasty, unhappy people (which you can politely point out as for example, asking the reader to click on the reviewer's name and see all their other negative reviews to realize that this is just a negative person). Or, the person wasn't a good fit for your business (so explain why). Or the person is being plain crazy. For example, I have had plastic surgeons condemned on Yelp because their waiting room was too hot, or other clients condemned because they didn't respond to an email. Finally, if the review is fake (i.e., by a competitor) or obscene or racist, you can complain to Yelp, Google+, etc., and in some cases they will remove the reviews. (To do this, log in to a personal account on Yelp, and right click on the offensive review. You can then flag it and complain).

To read Yelp's official guide to responding to reviews, visit http://jmlinks.com/5e. To read Google's, visit http://jmlinks.com/5f. To read TripAdvisor's, visit http://jmlinks.com/5g. For whatever review site matters to your business, you can usually search their help files for advice on how to respond to reviews. However, remember that the official policies are often very naive about how the game is truly played.

SWAMP NEGATIVE REVIEWS WITH POSITIVE REVIEWS

Again, in no way shape or form, am I advising you to be dishonest or solicit fake reviews. I am simply advising you to ask happy customers to just take a few minutes and tell their happy stories. If you pro-actively solicit positive, real reviews you can drown out or swamp the negative reviews with a preponderance of positive reviews. In short, getting positive real reviews is the best way to respond to negative reviews.

You don't ask, you don't get.

For your fourth TODO, download the **Review Solicitation Worksheet**. For the worksheet, go to https://www.jm-seo.org/workbooks (click on Yelp / Local, enter the code 'reviews2016' to register if you have not already done so), and click on the link to the "Reviews Solicitation Worksheet." You'll create a strategy to encourage positive reviews about your company.

» MONITOR AND IMPROVE YOUR ONLINE REPUTATION

Reputation management is a new buzzword about protecting one's online reputation, whether for an individual or a business. To understand reputation management, first back up and consider the sales funnel, often explained as *AIDA: Awareness, Interest, Desire and Action.* Prospective customers go through distinct phases as they consider solutions for their problems, needs, or desires:

Awareness. An **awareness** of the problem and the beginning of Internet searches and social media outreach to friends, family, and colleagues about the problem, need, or desire and possible solutions. In this phases, searches are often "educational" in nature as in "how to cater a wedding" or "wedding ideas."

Interest. As a customer becomes aware of available market solutions, they develop an **interest** in vendor offerings, and even may make a shortlist. At this stage, and the next, they move closer to an "action," i.e. a purchase or engagement with a vendor solution. Searches at this point become "best wedding caterers" or "Boston catering companies," etc.

Desire. Interest shifts towards **desire**, and the customer begins to narrow down his or her shortlist. At this point, searches become *reputational* in nature. They may search a business name PLUS words like *reviews* or *complaints*. If your business were named Gina's Italian Kitchen, for example. They might search Google for "Gina's Italian Kitchen Reviews" or "Complaints against Gina's Italian Kitchen," or "Gina's Italian Kitchen Wedding Catering Reviews." **Reviews** is the operative word; if he or she finds *positive* reviews, that confirms your business is a good choice, whereas if he or she finds *negative* reviews, they may take you out of the consideration set entirely.

Action. A choice is made to purchase the service or engage with your business. Upon completion, the customer may decide to leave her own review about your business for others.

Reputation management, in short, is monitoring and protecting your online **branded** and **reputational** searches. To be frank, it is also about attempting to upgrade positive reviews and positive brand mentions so that your online brand image shines.

To understand the search patterns, you can use the example of my company, The JM Internet Group. For example –

> a "branded" search is: "JM Internet Group"

> a "reputational" search is "JM Internet Group Reviews"

Review sites such as Yelp, CitySearch, Google+, etc., as well as ones specific to your industry can have an extremely positive – or extremely negative – impact on your online reputation. Indeed, branded searches on Google (searches for your company name, or your company name plus 'reviews') often return Google+ profiles and reviews directly on the right side of the page. For example, here's a screenshot for the search "JM Internet Group" on Google:

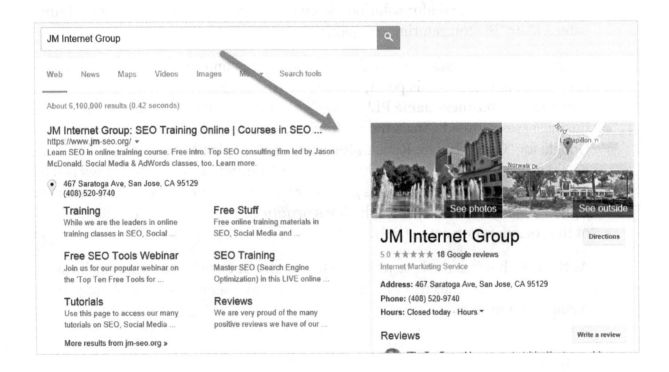

You can try the search at http://jmlinks.com/4v/. Notice the primacy of reviews and the highlighted Google+ listing information plus review count on the far right. If the search is for "JM Internet Group Reviews" at http://jmlinks.com/4w, notice that the No. 2 search result is Yelp, with the Better Business Bureau also on the page.

For a truly local business like a Pizza restaurant, even more local sites will be returned. For example, a search with respect to the very popular "Joe Momma" pizza restaurant in Tulsa at http://jmlinks.com/4w as "Joe Mommas reviews" has Yelp in positions No. 1, and 2, followed by zomato.com, and tripadvisor.com, both review sites.

Local review sites, in other words, are critical components of your online reputation management strategy. Google+ in particular can give you the marketer control of the branded search and the impressive right-hand side of the page, including photos. Check out a search for Joe Mommas Tulsa at http://jmlinks.com/4y.

In addition to identifying, claiming, and optimizing your business listings on relevant review sites, you should also monitor your business on these sites. Usually the act of claiming your listing in and of itself will generate an email any time someone reviews your company. Paid services such as ReviewPush (https://www.reviewpush.com/), Free Review Monitoring (https://freereviewmonitoring.com/), and ReviewTrackers (http://www.reviewtrackers.com/) are sophisticated alert systems so that you always know whenever a new review is published about your business.

For your fifth TODO, at a minimum set up a monthly checkup of your listings on the major review sites you have identified. Note in a spreadsheet how many reviews you have, how many are 5, 4, 3, 2, or 1 stars. If you have budget, consider using a paid monitoring service.

≫ MEASURE YOUR RESULTS

Reviews impact your business in two important ways:

- as a positive (or negative) "trust indicator" that you are a trustworthy business partner; and
- as a signal to search engines and review sites that you should rank high on searches for relevant keywords.

Reviews, in short, communicate that you are a "smart choice" and they propel you to the "top of search" whether that search is on Google, on Yelp, on TripAdvisor or on any other relevant review site.

MONITOR YOUR REVIEWS

Measurement of reviews, therefore, is focused on these two variables. On your keyword worksheet, I recommend that you create a tab called "local." Then every month, create a line item (for example, February 2016), note down for your business:

The review site, number of reviews you have, and cumulative star rating.

Secondly, try searches for your strategic keywords on Yelp, Google and/or on other relevant review sites (e.g., Airbnb, TripAdvisor, etc.), create a line item for each month, and indicate your position on those searches. For example, Andolino's Pizzeria was measured as No. 2 for the Google Search "pizza Tulsa" as seen in this screenshot on September 12, 2015.

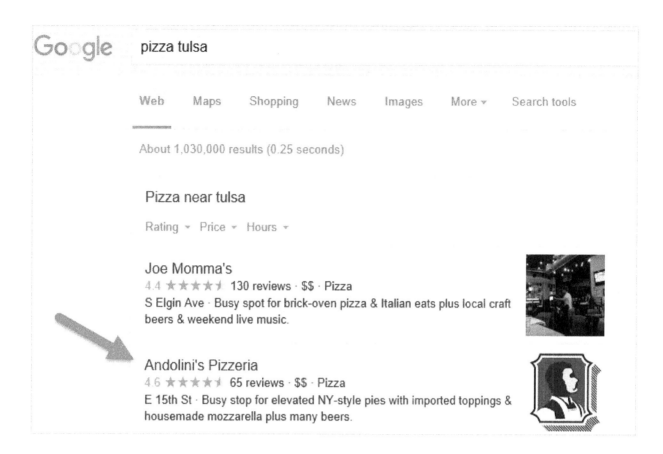

On Yelp, Andolini's is listed as No. 1. In other words, the restaurant is in good shape on both review sites. If it had dipped to a lower position on Yelp, for instance, then a Todo would be to encourage more Yelp reviews.

The two major aspects of monitoring your reviews, therefore are 1) your review count on each review site, and 2) your position on keyword searches on those sites. To the extent possible, you can then accelerate your efforts for a lagging site and relax a bit for a site for which you rank well and have positive reviews.

» DELIVERABLE: A YELP / LOCAL MARKETING PLAN

Now that we've come to the end our chapter on local reviews, your DELIVERABLE has arrived. For your final TODO, download the **Yelp / Local Marketing Plan Worksheet**. For the worksheet, go to https://www.jm-seo.org/workbooks (click on Yelp / Local, enter the code 'reviews2016' to register if you have not already done so), and click on the link to the "Yelp / Local Review Marketing Worksheet." By filling out this plan, you and your team will establish a vision of what you want to achieve via local reviews.

➤ TOP TEN LOCAL YELP / LOCAL MARKETING TOOLS AND RESOURCES

Here are the top ten tools and resources to help you with local review marketing. For an up-to-date list, go to https://www.jm-seo.org/workbooks (click on Yelp / Local, enter the code 'reviews2016' to register if you have not already done so), and click on the link to the *Social Media Toolbook* link, and drill down to the local reviews chapter.

GOOGLE MY BUSINESS (GOOGLE+ LOCAL / GOOGLE PLACES) HELP CENTER - https://support.google.com/business#topic=4539639

A wonderful and rather hidden microsite in the Googleplex with many help topics to learn about, modify, and update your Google+ Local listings. Google Local begot Google Places begot Google+ Local begot Google My Business. You and I both wish Google would settle on a name for its local service!

Rating: 5 Stars | **Category:** resource

MOZ LOCAL - https://moz.com/local

If local matters to you, you need to see where you're listed (Google+, Yelp, etc.), and how you're listed. You also want consistent address, phone number, and other data across local sites (called 'citations'). Moz has a new paid service for this, but this free tool will analyze (and find) your listings pretty easily.

Rating: 5 Stars | **Category:** tool

YELP SUPPORT CENTER (FOR BUSINESS OWNERS) - http://www.yelp-support.com/Yelp_for_Business_Owners?l=en_US

Yelp's site to support both users and businesses. As a business owner, click on the links to the left, or on 'Yelp for Business Owners' card. It's better than nothing, but Yelp still has a long way to go to be easy-to-use for business owners. Easy password reset?

Rating: 4 Stars | **Category:** resource

CITATION BUILDING STRATEGIES - THE COMPLETE LIST FOR LOCAL BUSINESSES - http://localstampede.com/citation-building-strategies-list

> It's always great when someone has done the brainstorming for you. If you are a local business, local 'citations' or links are incredibly helpful.
>
> **Rating:** 4 Stars | **Category:** article

LOCAL SEARCH RANKING FACTORS - http://davidmihm.com/local-search-ranking-factors.shtml

> An excellent yearly survey of factors that influence local search and SEO. Scroll about half way down the page, and look at the survey / factor list. Then brainstorm ways to make your company exhibit the factors as required. Some are easy (city and state in TITLE tag), others not so much: getting closer to the city center, getting more reviews.
>
> **Rating:** 4 Stars | **Category:** article

BEST LOCAL CITATIONS BY CATEGORY - http://moz.com/learn/local/citations-by-category

> If you're 'into local,' then you gotta know your citation sources. Obviously, Google+ is the most important for Google, and in many markets Yelp is #2. But for a plumber vs. a chiropractor, where to get citations (listings on local sites) can be different. Moz breaks out the 'best' citation sources by common category.
>
> **Rating:** 4 Stars | **Category:** article

LOCAL KEYWORD LIST GENERATOR - http://5minutesite.com/local_keywords.php

> Don't know your local geography? What about all those pesky zip codes and small suburban towns? Enter a zip code or city into this tool, and it generates a nifty list of possible nearby locales and zips for your SEO efforts. A time saver if local search is important to your SEO.
>
> **Rating:** 3 Stars | **Category:** tool

BRIGHTLOCAL REVIEWBIZ WIDGET - http://brightlocal.com/seo-tools/review-biz

Technically not a free tool, but getting reviews is so important, and this little widget makes an all-in-one how to ask for a review widget.

Rating: 3 Stars | **Category:** tool

GOOGLE REVIEW HANDOUT GENERATOR - http://whitespark.ca/review-handout-generator

This very slick tool allows you to input your company, website, and logo and then it generates a very nice-looking PDF / handout you can give your clients and thereby solicit Google reviews. The PDF is very well done.

Rating: 3 Stars | **Category:** tool

GEOSITEMAPGENERATOR - http://geositemapgenerator.com

This doesn't really generate a sitemap. Rather it tells Google and Bing your physical address, which is a useful signal for local SEO.

Rating: 1 Stars | **Category:** tool

YELP LOCAL TOOLS

Yelp, Google+, and other local review sites have a cornucopia of free resources and free tools to make your life easier. Below I produce my favorite tools and resources (in rank order). Remember that by registering your copy of the workbook, you can access the Social Media Toolbook, which has all the tools in convenient, clickable PDF format. To register, go to https://www.jm-seo.org/workbooks (click on Yelp / Local, enter the code 'reviews2016' to register if you have not already done so), and click on the link to the *Social Media Toolbook*.

Here are free Yelp / Google+ / Local tools and resources, sorted with the best items first.

GOOGLE MY BUSINESS (GOOGLE+ LOCAL / GOOGLE PLACES) HELP CENTER - https://support.google.com/business#topic=4539639

> A wonderful and rather hidden microsite in the Googleplex with many help topics to learn about, modify, and update your Google+ Local listings. Google Local begot Google Places begot Google+ Local begot Google My Business. You and I both wish Google would settle on a name for its local service!

> **Rating:** 5 Stars | **Category:** resource

INSIDER PAGES - http://insiderpages.com

> Insider Pages enables people to find local businesses through recommendations from friends and neighbors. Users can create and share reviews of local businesses and perform detailed searches for businesses across the country in numerous categories.

Rating: 5 Stars | **Category:** service

Moz Local - https://moz.com/local

If local matters to you, you need to see where you're listed (Google+, Yelp, etc.), and how you're listed. You also want consistent address, phone number, and other data across local sites (called 'citations'). Moz has a new paid service for this, but this free tool will analyze (and find) your listings pretty easily.

Rating: 5 Stars | **Category:** tool

Bing Places for Business (Bing Local) - http://bingplaces.com

Bing is a distant #2 to Google, behind probably Yahoo...but nonetheless, for local search purposes, it's still valuable to find (and claim) your local listing on Bing Local. So go for it, be a Binger!

Rating: 5 Stars | **Category:** service

Yelp - http://biz.yelp.com

Yelp is a local reviews service. Businesses can have (and claim) a FREE listing on Yelp, which can be helpful for local listings and local link building. This link is to the 'business' portal at Yelp - how to find, and list your business.

Rating: 5 Stars | **Category:** service

Citysearch - http://citysearch.com

Citysearch is a local guide for better city living. It covers thousands of locations nationwide, and combines editorial recommendations, user comments, and expert advice to keep you connected to popular and undiscovered places. It has a search tool to find businesses and services with integrated reviews. Make sure to check if you're listed and encourage good reviews.

Rating: 5 Stars | **Category:** service

Google My Business (Google Local / Google Places) -
http://google.com/business

> Google My Business is the new official name, but behind-the-scenes they still call it Google Places or Google Local or Google+ Local. Or whatchamacallit. This is the official entry point to find and claim your small business listing on Google's local service.
>
> **Rating:** 5 Stars | **Category:** resource

Yelp Support Center (For Business Owners) - http://www.yelp-support.com/Yelp_for_Business_Owners?l=en_US

> Yelp's site to support both users and businesses. As a business owner, click on the links to the left, or on 'Yelp for Business Owners' card. It's better than nothing, but Yelp still has a long way to go to be easy-to-use for business owners. Easy password reset?
>
> **Rating:** 4 Stars | **Category:** resource

Yahoo! Local - http://local.yahoo.com

> Yahoo! Local is a comprehensive business directory for cities in the USA and Canada complete with ratings and reviews, maps, events, and more. Find or include your business for help not just with Yahoo but with local search on Bing and Google.
>
> **Rating:** 4 Stars | **Category:** service

Citation Building Strategies - The Complete List For Local Businesses -
http://localstampede.com/citation-building-strategies-list

> It's always great when someone has done the brainstorming for you. If you are a local business, local 'citations' or links are incredibly helpful.
>
> **Rating:** 4 Stars | **Category:** article

Local Search Ranking Factors - http://davidmihm.com/local-search-ranking-factors.shtml

An excellent yearly survey of factors that influence local search and SEO. Scroll about half way down the page, and look at the survey / factor list. Then brainstorm ways to make your company exhibit the factors as required. Some are easy (city and state in TITLE tag), others not so much: getting closer to the city center, getting more reviews.

Rating: 4 Stars | **Category:** article

GOOGLE MAPS (FIND YOUR GOOGLE PLACES LISTING) -
https://www.google.com/maps/

Confusingly, Google Maps is where you go to sign in and thereby write reviews about local businesses for Google. Thank you search engine giant for - yet again - making something so difficult to find! Use this to find your listing easily. You can also build maps for customers.

Rating: 4 Stars | **Category:** service

GOOGLE AND YOUR BUSINESS HELP FORUM -
http://productforums.google.com/forum/#!forum/business

Forums by people using Google Places, er Google and Your Business. You can get help from the community here, which is often more effective than those annoying canned emails you get from Google itself!

Rating: 4 Stars | **Category:** resource

SMALL BUSINESS GUIDE TO GOOGLE MY BUSINESS -
http://simplybusiness.co.uk/microsites/google-my-business-guide

Interactive step-by-step flowchart to using Google My Business. Comprised of key questions and linked resources with more information. Chart is divided into different areas including setup, page management and optimization, engagement and reviews, and citations.

Rating: 4 Stars | **Category:** resource

GOOGLE PLACES CATEGORIES - http://blumenthals.com/google-lbc-categories

When setting up your free listing on Google Places, be sure to choose categories that are already existing. Use this to tool help you identify extant categories as you work on your five free categories for Google Places. Perform a search by entering a term or click the search button.

Rating: 4 Stars | **Category:** tool

BEST LOCAL CITATIONS BY CATEGORY - http://moz.com/learn/local/citations-by-category

If you're 'into local,' then you gotta know your citation sources. Obviously, Google+ is the most important for Google, and in many markets Yelp is #2. But for a plumber vs. a chiropractor, where to get citations (listings on local sites) can be different. Moz breaks out the 'best' citation sources by common category.

Rating: 4 Stars | **Category:** article

YEXT - http://www.yext.com/

Follow the instructions to 'scan your business.' This nifty tool allows you to input your business name and phone number and it will go out and find all the relevant listings across many, many different local listings services. Then you can (pay) to have it fix many of them. Not perfect, but a good start on identifying logical local listing opportunities for your business.

Rating: 4 Stars | **Category:** tool

GOOGLE STRUCTURED DATA MARKUP HELPER - https://google.com/webmasters/markup-helper

Structured data, or microdata, allows Google and other search engines to know if you have an event with dates, a picture you want as your logo, or even a recipe calorie count. Very useful for local search optimization. Use this free tool to generate the required markup.

Rating: 4 Stars | **Category:** tool

YAHOO LOCALWORKS - https://smallbusiness.yahoo.com/localworks

Citations - mentions of your company, address, and phone number across many local listing sites - have a big impact on your rank on Google and Bing. This nifty tool from Yahoo allows you to input your business name, phone, address, and zip and get a report on where you are already indexed, and how.

Rating: 4 Stars | **Category:** service

GOOGLE MY BUSINESS (GOOGLE PLACES / GOOGLE LOCAL) HELP CENTER -
https://support.google.com/business

Help with Google Places, conveniently hidden by Google..but here is where you can browse helpful articles on setting up and managing your free advertising and promotion efforts via Google Places.

Rating: 4 Stars | **Category:** resource

LOCAL KEYWORD LIST GENERATOR - http://5minutesite.com/local_keywords.php

Don't know your local geography? What about all those pesky zip codes and small suburban towns? Enter a zip code or city into this tool, and it generates a nifty list of possible nearby locales and zips for your SEO efforts. A time saver if local search is important to your SEO.

Rating: 3 Stars | **Category:** tool

BRIGHTLOCAL REVIEWBIZ WIDGET - http://brightlocal.com/seo-tools/review-biz

Technically not a free tool, but getting reviews is so important, and this little widget makes an all-in-one how to ask for a review widget.

Rating: 3 Stars | **Category:** tool

SCHEMA.ORG 'LOCAL' SCHEMA CREATOR - http://51blocks.com/checklists-tools/schema-creator

If you are a local business and easily can add HTML code to your site, you can use this tool to generate structured data to enable search engines to better 'understand' you.

Rating: 3 Stars | **Category:** tool

MICROFORMATS CODE & TOOLS - http://microformats.org/wiki/code-tools

Microdata, rich snippets, microformats - whatever you call them they are important! For local search, you want to 'tell' Google / Bing your location. This page gives you the ability to generate that code for your webpages, free.

Rating: 3 Stars | **Category:** tool

ULTIMATE GUIDE TO MICROFORMATS: REFERENCE AND EXAMPLES - http://sixrevisions.com/web-development/ultimate-guide-to-microformats-reference-and-examples

Microdata, rich snippets, microformats - whatever you call them they are important. If you aren't familiar with microformats, this article is a great introduction.

Rating: 3 Stars | **Category:** article

GOOGLE REVIEW HANDOUT GENERATOR - http://whitespark.ca/review-handout-generator

This very slick tool allows you to input your company, website, and logo and then it generates a very nice-looking PDF / handout you can give your clients and thereby solicit Google reviews. The PDF is very well done.

Rating: 3 Stars | **Category:** tool

YELP BLOG FOR BUSINESS OWNERS - https://biz.yelp.com/blog

If local SEO / local SMM / Yelp matters to you, well, you MUST subscribe to and follow the official Yelp blog. Take it all with a grain of salt and a good dose of skepticism, as it is the OFFICIAL blog, so it gives you a good dose of Yelp-is-so-fantastic propaganda, but it is the official source.

Rating: 3 Stars | **Category:** blog

LocalVox - http://localvox.com/free-report

Find out if, and where, your local business is listed. Then go and get listed!

Rating: 3 Stars | **Category:** service

Extending HTML5 — Microformats - http://html5doctor.com/microformats/

If you're anything like my amazing 20 year old daughter, you have no idea what microformats are. Well, never fear, HTML5 Doctor has you covered. This article is an extensive introduction into microformats and provides everything you need to know (and more).

Rating: 2 Stars | **Category:** article

Yelp Advertiser FAQ - http://yelp.com/advertiser_faq

Many business owners hate Yelp. In fact, hate might be a mild word. Here is Yelp's side of the story, responding to criticism of their review system. Take it with a grain of salt: it is Yelp's side of the story, but it has interesting factoids in it, such as how incredibly powerful negative reviews can affect your business.

Rating: 2 Stars | **Category:** article

GeoSiteMapGenerator - http://geositemapgenerator.com

This doesn't really generate a sitemap. Rather it tells Google and Bing your physical address, which is a useful signal for local SEO.

Rating: 1 Stars | **Category:** tool

Yelp Webinars for Business - https://biz.yelp.com/blog/upcoming-webinar-schedule-2

Yelp produces OFFICIAL webinars not only on Yelp advertising but on how to create a good free listing. All of this with the caveat that they only tell you the official stuff, not the secret tips and tricks, but still worth while.

Rating: 1 Stars | **Category:** blog

www.ingramcontent.com/pod-product-compliance
Lightning Source LLC
Chambersburg PA
CBHW060443060326
40690CB00019B/4311